# Poems From The Works Of William Cullen Bryant

Bryant, William Cullen, 1794-1878, Hodgdon, Josephine E., comp

𝕷𝖊𝖆𝖋𝖑𝖊𝖙𝖘 ....𝖆𝖓𝖉𝖆𝖗𝖉 𝕬𝖚𝖙𝖍𝖔𝖗𝖘.

# BRYANT.

## POEMS FROM THE
## WORKS OF WILLIAM CULLEN BRYANT,

*FOR HOMES, LIBRARIES, AND SCHOOLS.*

COMPILED BY
JOSEPHINE E. HODGDON.

*ILLUSTRATED.*

NEW YORK:
D. APPLETON AND COMPANY,
1902.

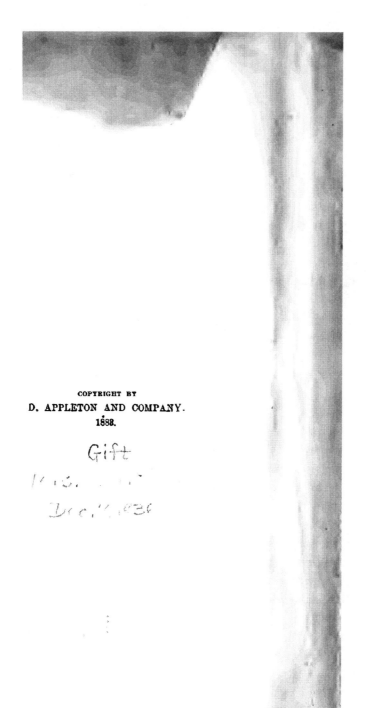

# CONTENTS.

| | PAGE |
|---|---|
| WILLIAM CULLEN BRYANT | 7 |
| THANATOPSIS | 15 |
| THE YELLOW VIOLET | 17 |
| TO A WATERFOWL | 19 |
| INSCRIPTION FOR THE ENTRANCE TO A WOOD | 21 |
| THE WEST WIND | 23 |
| OCTOBER | 25 |
| NOVEMBER | 26 |
| A FOREST HYMN | 27 |
| THE FIRMAMENT | 31 |
| THE GLADNESS OF NATURE | 33 |
| "I BROKE THE SPELL THAT HELD ME LONG" | 34 |
| MIDSUMMER | 35 |
| WILLIAM TELL | 37 |
| TO THE FRINGED GENTIAN | 39 |
| "INNOCENT CHILD AND SNOW-WHITE FLOWER" | 41 |
| THE TWENTY-SECOND OF DECEMBER | 43 |
| THOU, GOD, SEEST ME | 44 |
| SEVENTY-SIX | 45 |
| THE BATTLE OF BENNINGTON | 46 |
| THE ANTIQUITY OF FREEDOM | 47 |
| THE WHITE-FOOTED DEER | 51 |
| THE LAND OF DREAMS | 53 |
| THE PLANTING OF THE APPLE-TREE | 55 |
| THE SNOW-SHOWER | 57 |
| ROBERT OF LINCOLN | 59 |

iv

PAGE

A Song of New-Year's Eve . . . . . . . . . 61

The Little People of the Snow . . . . . . . 63

Abraham Lincoln . . . . . . . . . . . 77

A Legend of St. Martin . . . . . . . . . 79

The Words of the Koran . . . . . . . . . 81

The Mystery of Flowers . . . . . . . . . 83

The Centennial Hymn . . . . . . . . . . 85

The Flood of Years . . . . . . . . . 87

In Memory of John Lothrop Motley . . . . . 91

The Twenty-second of February . . . . . . . 93

Fables: . . . . . . . . . . . . 94

The Elm and the Vine.
The Donkey and the Mocking-Bird.
The Caterpillar and the Butterfly.
The Spider's Web.
The Dial and the Sun.
The Eagle and the Serpent.
The Woodman and the Sandal-Tree.
The Hidden Rill.
The Cost of a Pleasure.

# INTRODUCTION TO THE LEAFLETS.

"Consider what you have in the smallest chosen library. A company of the wisest and wittiest men that could be picked out of all civil countries, in a thousand years, have set in best order the results of their learning and wisdom. The men themselves were hid and inaccessible, solitary, impatient of interruptions, fenced by etiquette; but the thought which they did not uncover to their bosom friend is here written out in transparent words to us, the strangers of another age."—RALPH WALDO EMERSON.

How can our young people be led to take pleasure in the writings of our best authors?

An attempt to answer this important inquiry is the aim of these *Leaflets*. It is proposed, by their use in the school and the family, to develop a love for the beautiful thoughts, the noble and elevating sentiments, that pervade the choicest literature, and thus to turn aside that flood of pernicious reading which is deluging the children of our beloved country. It is hoped that they will prove effective instruments in securing the desired end, and an aid in the attainment of a higher mental and moral culture.

Our best writers, intelligent teachers, and lecturers on literary subjects, have given suggestions and material for this work, and rendered its realization possible. Those who, knowing the power of a good thought well expressed, have endeavored to popularize works of acknowledged merit by means of copied extracts, marked passages, leaves torn from books, and other expensive and time-consuming expedients, will gladly welcome this new, convenient, and inexpensive arrangement of appropriate selections as helps to the progress they are attempting to secure. This plan and the selections used are the outgrowth of experience in the school-room, and their utility and adaptation to the proposed aims have been proved. By means of these sheets, each teacher can have at command a larger range of authors than is otherwise possible. A few suggestions in regard to these Leaflets may not be amiss:

1. They may be used for sight-reading and silent reading.

2. They may be employed for analysis of the author's meaning and language, which may well be made a prominent feature of the reading-lesson, as it is the best preparation for a proper rendering of the passages given.

3. They may be distributed, that each pupil may spend any spare time in choosing his own favorite selection. This may afterward be used, as its character or the pupil's inclination suggests, for sentiment, essay, reading, recitation, or declamation.

4. Mr. Longfellow's method, as mentioned in the sketch accompanying

his poems, in this series of Leaflets, may be profitably followed, as it will promote a helpful interplay of thought between teacher and pupils, and lead unconsciously to a love and understanding of good authors.

5. Short quotations may be given in answer to the daily roll-call.

6. Some of the selections are especially adapted to responsive and chorus class-reading.

7. The lyrical poems can be sung to some familiar tunes.

8. The sketch which will be found with each series may serve as the foundation for essays on the author's life and works.

9. The illustrations may be employed as subjects for language-lessons, thus cultivating the powers of observation and expression.

All these methods combined may be made to give pleasure to the pupils' friends, and make it feasible to entertain them oftener than is now the custom, thus creating an interest in the school and a sympathy with the author whose works are the subjects of study. The foregoing is by no means a necessary order, and teachers will vary from it as their own appreciation of the intelligence of their pupils and the interest of the exercise shall suggest.

The object to be kept in view is, pleasantly to introduce the works of our best authors to growing minds, and to develop in them a taste for the best in literature, that the world of books may become to them an unfailing source of inspiration and delight.

# LEAFLETS FROM STANDARD AUTHORS.

## WILLIAM CULLEN BRYANT.

*William Cullen Bryant*

A FEW years ago there died in New York city a man standing in the first rank of literature, who had made his literary reputation before Sir Walter Scott began his series of the Waverley novels. He was in his prime when Dickens and Thackeray first began to write, and in the full exercise of his intellectual powers after they had laid aside forever their busy

7

pens. Closely identified with the national life of his native land, and having a large share in originating and elevating its literature, and in shaping the course of its politics, William Cullen Bryant truly merited the encomium of being accounted "the most accomplished, the most distinguished, and the most universally honored, citizen of the United States," and that, too, solely by his genius, moral rectitude, and force of character. "He was my master in verse," said Longfellow, "ten years and more my senior, and throughout my whole life I have had the warmest reverential regard for him." "It is certain," said Ralph Waldo Emerson, "that Bryant has written some of the very best poetry that we have had in America." Bryant was born in Cummington, a little town in Western Massachusetts, on November 3, 1794. His father, Dr. Peter Bryant, was a man of rare intelligence, taste, and sagacity, a practicing physician and surgeon, and one of the third generation who had followed that profession. The genial doctor never realized his dream of educating a child of his own for his favorite profession. He named the future poet and journalist after Dr. Cullen, the famous Scotch physician, but William never had any liking for his father's profession, realizing fully, as he said in after-years, the unremitting toil and arduous duties of a country doctor's life. William Cullen's mother was a lineal descendant of John Alden, the lieutenant of Miles Standish and the hero of one of Longfellow's charming poems. She was a woman of great force of character, of personal dignity, and excellent good sense. Although her education was limited to the ordinary English branches, she was a great reader, and early taught her child to repeat standard English poetry. When he was scarcely three years old, William was made to repeat Dr. Watts's psalms and hymns. In his poem called "A Lifetime," written when the scenes of childhood were memories of the long past, Bryant pictures himself standing by his mother's knee and repeating some of Dr. Watts's devotional verses. In a charming article, written when the poet was eighty-two years old, for a leading juvenile magazine, and also in the fragment of an autobiography, printed in Mr. Parke Godwin's Life, Bryant has given the world the story of his boyish days. He tells us of the system of family discipline which parents thought necessary in order to secure obedience, and of the respect paid by the young to their seniors, especially to ministers of the gospel. Of the books to which he had access, eighty years ago, he tells us, some were excellent and some were trash or worse; among the good he names "Sandford and Merton," "Robinson Crusoe," "Pilgrim's Progress," Mrs. Barbauld's works, Watts's and Cowper's poems. From a very early age, Bryant displayed a taste for reading and study. His father took great pains to direct his boy to those great English classics of which he had been a life-long student. The lad delighted to pore over Pope, Gray, and Goldsmith, and soon began to write verses. The varied and picturesque scenery of Western Massachusetts became familiar to him from his love of out-door life and the companionship of his father. Thus even from childhood his native hills, valleys, woods, and rivers, were like old friends, and he was taught to love Nature under all her varied aspects. A man of sound scholarship and refined tastes, Dr. Bryant, recognizing the poetic gift of his son, judiciously and wisely aided in its development. While he encouraged the first rude efforts of boyish genius and taught the value of correctness and compression, he also trained his son "to distinguish between true poetic enthusiasm and fustian." Even from the first, there was nothing forced, morbid, or immature about the young poet's verses; and he wrote as if he had already had experience. Bryant's poetical powers, thus early developed, remained unimpaired to an age beyond that usually allotted to man. "Thanatopsis" was written in his eighteenth year; and the noble "Ode" written for Washington's birthday, February 22, 1878, in his eighty-fourth. Hence, an eminent scholar has justly said: "No one will deny that in one respect, at least, Bryant's fame was entirely unique. He was the author of the finest verses ever produced by any one so young, and so old, as the author of 'Thanatopsis' and of 'The Twenty-second of February.'"

In 1807 President Jefferson laid an embargo on American shipping, an act which was bitterly denounced in New England. The boy Bryant caught the spirit of the times and made the hated embargo the subject of a satirical poem, entitled "The Embargo; or, Sketches of the Times," which was published in Boston in 1808, "by a youth of thirteen." The poem was favorably received, and a second edition called for. During the next few years several other poems were written, undoubtedly clever, but by no means characteristic of the poet's subsequent productions. In 1810, in his sixteenth year, Bryant entered Williams College, and remained there for two years, but was obliged to leave on account of his father's pecuniary affairs, which rendered retrenchment necessary. Dr. Bryant intended to send his son back to college, but was unable to do so. Of Bryant's brief collegiate career many interesting particulars have been recorded. He distinguished himself for his aptness and industry in the study of the ancient classics and his love for the best literature. The college afterward conferred upon him the degree of A. M., and enrolled him as an alumnus. After leaving college Bryant continued his studies at home for a time, but soon began the study of law, first with Judge Howe, of Worthington, near Cummington, and afterward with Mr. William Baylies, of Bridgewater. In 1815, at the age of twenty-one, he was admitted to the bar. He first opened an office at Plainfield, but after a time settled in Great Barrington. In the latter place he passed the next nine years of his life, and there some of his well-known poems were written. When the young poet went away from his native town to read law, he left the manuscript of a poem behind him, which was found by his father and sent by him to the "North American Review." One of the editors, Richard H. Dana, read the poem carefully, and was so surprised at its excellence that he doubted whether it was written on this side of the Atlantic. This remarkable poem, known to all the world as "Thanatopsis," was printed in the "North American Review" for September, 1817. "This poem," says George William Curtis, "was the first adequate poetic voice of the solemn New England spirit. Moreover, it was without a harbinger in our literature, and without a trace of the English masters of the hour." A pleasant story is told, that when the poet's father showed "Thanatopsis" in manuscript to a lady well qualified to judge of its merits, simply saying, "Oh! read that—it is Cullen's," she read the poem, raised her eyes to the good doctor's face, and burst into tears, in which the father, a reserved and silent man, was not ashamed to join. Six months later, in March, 1818, the young poet added to his reputation by publishing a poem entitled "To a Waterfowl," in the "North American Review." This exquisite piece, written in clear and strong language, in melody simple and sweet, and displaying a keen and accurate observation of nature, has always been a favorite, and displays some of Bryant's best characteristics.

In 1821 Mr. Bryant was married to Miss Frances Fairchild, and for nearly half a century she was the good angel of his life. During all these years "his wife was his only really intimate friend, and when she died he had no other. He was young, his fame was growing, and with domestic duties, with literary studies and work, and professional and public activities, his tranquil days passed in the happy valley of the Housatonic." It was to his wife that Bryant addressed the poem beginning, "O fairest of the rural maids," "The Future Life," and "The Life that Is"; and her memory and her loss are tenderly embalmed in one of the most touching of his later poems, "October, 1866." On account of the interest awakened by his published poems, and through the influence of Mr. Dana, Bryant was invited to deliver a poem before the Phi Beta Kappa Society at Harvard College, an honor rarely conferred upon so young a man. He accepted, and read at Cambridge, in 1821, the longest and most elaborate poem he ever wrote, entitled "The Ages." Richard H. Stoddard describes it as "a rapid, comprehensive, philosophic, and picturesque summary of the history of mankind from the earliest periods, a shifting panorama of good and evil figures and deeds, the rising and falling of religions, kingdoms, empires, and the great shapes of Greece and Rome." Thoughtful and suggestive, it stands first in all the complete editions of Bryant's collected works, forming a fitting introduction to the other poems. The next four years of the young poet's life were more productive than any before, for some thirty of his best poems were written during this time. In the mean time a little thin book of forty-four pages, containing "The Ages" and others of his poems, had been published, and was everywhere favorably received. It established beyond question his reputation as a poet. By this time, it became generally known that Bryant disliked his profession, and would welcome any relief from its irksome duties. Influential friends secured a literary position for him in New York city, and early in 1825 he left the Berkshire hills for the more congenial occupation of journalism in the great metropolis. "Here he lived," says his intimate friend James Grant Wilson, "from earliest youth to venerable age —from thirty-one to eighty-four—in one path of honor and success." In 1826 Bryant became permanently connected with the "Evening Post," with which his name was associated until the day of his death—more than half a century afterward. To his future life-work of journalism the young editor brought literary experience, solid learning, refined taste, and, even then, the prestige of a well-earned reputation. Bryant was too wise a man to suppose that poetry would ever give him a substantial living. "I should have starved," he once said, "if I had been obliged to depend upon my poetry for a living." As a newspaper editor and proprietor, he was a sagacious and successful man of business. Thrift and strict economy were cardinal virtues with him. He was thorough, watchful, and industrious in the smallest details of his newspaper work. He made the "Post" an educational power among its readers by diffusing scientific and practical information, and by stimulating the public mind to the enjoyment of literature and art. During at least forty-two of his fifty-two years of editorial service, Mr. Bryant was at his editorial desk before eight o'clock in the morning, and left the daily impress of his character and genius in some form upon the columns of his journal. These long years were most momentous in the history of this country, and were passed in active aggressive work in the very center of political, intellectual, and national activity. During all this time not only did no stain rest upon his character, but he stood as a conspicuous example of all that was admirable in journalism, in politics, and in private life. "He never engaged," said John Bigelow, in his address before the Century Club, "in any other business enterprise; he never embarked in any financial speculations; he was never an officer of any other financial or industrial corporation, nor did he ever accept any political office or trust."

While Bryant continued a journalist all the days of his long life, he never ceased to be a poet. He earned his bread and molded public opinion with his newspaper, but looked to poetry for the perpetuation of his name. He never confounded the two vocations in any way, or allowed either to interfere to any great extent with the other. In brief, he wrote his editorials in the office, and his poetry in the quiet of his home. If we take into account only what Bryant published in book form, he wrote comparatively little. If we reckon his editorial contributions to the "Post," during fifty-two years, we shall find him one of the most voluminous writers that ever lived. Some one, who had every opportunity to know, has estimated that his editorials alone would fill more than a hundred duodecimo volumes of five hundred pages each—all this, too, written in a style always pure, clear, and forcible, and giving evidence of wide scholarship and profound reflection. Under Bryant's sagacious and far-sighted management the "Post" became not only an influential and leading journal, but was also a financial success. Its editor died a wealthy man. As a rest from his arduous labors, Bryant traveled occasionally. Between the years 1834 and 1867 he made six visits to Europe, and

Cedarmere.

at different times made long journeys through his own country. His readers traced his travels by his letters to the "Evening Post," which attracted a deal of attention for their keen observation and beauty of expression. Mr. Bryant published occasional volumes of poetry made up of his contributions to the periodicals of the day; and in 1876 a complete illustrated edition of his poetical writings was issued. Under the heavy pressure of grief caused by the death of his beloved wife in 1866, the veteran poet at the age of seventy-two set himself to the formidable task of translating the "Iliad" and the "Odyssey." The former occupied most of his leisure for three years, and the latter about two. These translations were highly praised both at home and abroad. Mr. Bryant had the peculiar talent of delivering addresses and memorial orations upon the lives and works of eminent men. A volume of these felicitous and appreciative addresses was published in 1872. His last poem of any great length was "The Flood of Years," written in the poet's eighty-second year, and showing no decay of his poetic genius. The venerable poet's last public appearance was at the Central Park, in New York city, May 29, 1878, at the unveiling of a statue to Mazzini. After delivering his oration in the open air, and at times exposed to the hot rays of the sun, he walked to the home of his friend General Wilson. Just as he was about to enter the door, the aged poet fell suddenly, striking his head on the stone steps. He rallied somewhat and was able to ride to his own home. Paralysis of his right side followed, and, on July 12, 1878, his life, after sinking like a slowly-ebbing tide, came to a peaceful end.

The tributes paid to Bryant's genius by the press and the public generally were immediate, warm, and sincere. The memory of the beloved poet is deservedly enshrined in that universal esteem and admiration which his noble life, as well as his literary achievements, had won for him.

Mr. Bryant's wealth enabled him to live surrounded by every comfort and luxury. So far as he was personally concerned, he seemed to care very little for them. He had three residences, a city house in New York, a country house called "Cedarmere," at Roslyn, Long Island, and the old homestead of the Bryant family at Cummington, Massachusetts. Very few famous men were better known by sight than the veteran editor. Day after day, and year after year, he could be seen in all weathers walking down to his office in the morning, and back to his house in the afternoon. He kept his vigor of body and mind by temperate self-restraint, good sense, a rigid observance of the laws of health, both in regard to proper sanitary arrangements and a strict attention to diet, sleep, and exercise. He rose early—about half-past five in winter, and generally an hour earlier in summer. A series of light gymnastics lasting for an hour or more, together with a bath from head to foot, followed. His food was of the simplest kind. Hominy and milk, brown bread or oatmeal, with baked sweet apples and other fruit, made up his breakfast. For dinner, he ate a moderate quantity of meat or fish, but generally made his dinner mostly of vegetables. His supper consisted only of bread and butter and fruit. He never drank tea or coffee, and very rarely took a glass of wine. He always went to bed early—in town, as early as ten; in the country, somewhat earlier. Even in the worst weather he always preferred to walk rather than to ride. His senses were perfect, his eyes needed no glasses, and his hearing was exquisitely fine until the day of the accident. Well might those who knew him best say that, but for the accident which caused his death, he would probably have become a veritable centenarian.

Such was the pure, noble, and consistent life of William Cullen Bryant. His life and his grand life-work in literature all testify to his being truly and essentially a great and good man.

14

## THANATOPSIS.

To him who in the love of Nature holds
Communion with her visible forms, she speaks
A various language; for his gayer hours
She has a voice of gladness, and a smile
And eloquence of beauty, and she glides
Into his darker musings, with a mild
And healing sympathy, that steals away
Their sharpness, ere he is aware. When thoughts
Of the last bitter hour come like a blight
Over thy spirit, and sad images
Of the stern agony, and shroud, and pall,
And breathless darkness, and the narrow house,
Make thee to shudder, and grow sick at heart—
Go forth, under the open sky, and list
To Nature's teachings, while from all around—
Earth and her waters, and the depths of air—
Comes a still voice.—

   Yet a few days, and thee
The all-beholding sun shall see no more
In all his course; nor yet in the cold ground,
Where thy pale form was laid, with many tears,
Nor in the embrace of ocean, shall exist
Thy image. Earth, that nourished thee, shall claim
Thy growth, to be resolved to earth again,
And, lost each human trace, surrendering up
Thine individual being, shalt thou go
To mix forever with the elements,
To be a brother to the insensible rock
And to the sluggish clod, which the rude swain
Turns with his share, and treads upon. The oak
Shall send his roots abroad, and pierce thy mould.

 Yet not to thine eternal resting-place
Shalt thou retire alone, nor couldst thou wish
Couch more magnificent. Thou shalt lie down
With patriarchs of the infant world —with kings,
The powerful of the earth—the wise, the good,
Fair forms, and hoary seers of ages past,

All in one mighty sepulchre. The hills
Rock-ribbed and ancient as the sun—the vales
Stretching in pensive quietness between;
The venerable woods — rivers that move
In majesty, and the complaining brooks
That make the meadows green; and, poured round all,
Old Ocean's gray and melancholy waste—
Are but the solemn decorations all
Of the great tomb of man. The golden sun,
The planets, all the infinite host of heaven,
Are shining on the sad abodes of death,
Through the still lapse of ages. All that tread
The globe are but a handful to the tribes
That slumber in its bosom. Take the wings
Of morning, pierce the Barcan wilderness,
Or lose thyself in the continuous woods
Where rolls the Oregon, and hears no sound,
Save his own dashings—yet the dead are there:
And millions in those solitudes, since first
The flight of years began, have laid them down
In their last sleep—the dead reign there alone.
So shalt thou rest; and what if thou withdraw
In silence from the living, and no friend
Take note of thy departure? All that breathe
Will share thy destiny. The gay will laugh
When thou art gone, the solemn brood of care
Plod on, and each one as before will chase
His favorite phantom; yet all these shall leave
Their mirth and their employments, and shall come
And make their bed with thee. As the long train
Of ages glides away, the sons of men,
The youth in life's fresh spring, and he who goes
In the full strength of years, matron and maid,
The speechless babe, and the gray-headed man—
Shall one by one be gathered to thy side,
By those, who in their turn shall follow them.

So live, that when thy summons comes to join
The innumerable caravan, which moves
To that mysterious realm, where each shall take
His chamber in the silent halls of death,
Thou go not, like the quarry-slave at night,
Scourged to his dungeon, but, sustained and soothed
By an unfaltering trust, approach thy grave,
Like one who wraps the drapery of his couch
About him, and lies down to pleasant dreams.

## THE YELLOW VIOLET.

ᴡʜᴇɴ beechen buds begin to swell,
And woods the blue-bird's warble
     know,
A yellow violet's modest bell
Peeps from the last year's leaves
     below.

Ere russet fields their green resume,
Sweet flower, I love, in forest bare,

To meet thee, when thy faint per-
     fume
     Alone is in the virgin air.

Of all her train, the hands of Spring
     First plant thee in the watery
          mould,
And I have seen thee blossoming
     Beside the snow-bank's edges cold.

2                          17

Thy parent sun, who bade thee view,
  Pale skies, and chilling moisture
    sip,
Has bathed thee in his own bright
  hue,
  And streaked with jet thy glow-
    ing lip.

Yet slight thy form, and low thy seat,
  And earthward bent thy gentle eye,
Unapt the passing view to meet,
  When loftier flowers are flaunting
    nigh.

Oft, in the sunless April day,
  Thy early smile has stayed my
    walk;

But midst the gorgeous blooms of
  May,
  I passed thee on thy humble stalk.

So they, who climb to wealth, forget
  The friends in darker fortunes
    tried.
I copied them—but I regret
  That I should ape the ways of
    pride.

And when again the genial hour
  Awakes the painted tribes of light,
I'll not o'erlook the modest flower
  That made the woods of April
    bright.

## TO A WATERFOWL.

Whither, midst falling dew,
While glow the heavens with the last
    steps of day,
Far, through their rosy depths, dost
    thou pursue
    Thy solitary way?

Vainly the fowler's eye
Might mark thy distant flight to do
    thee wrong,
As, darkly painted on the crimson sky,
    Thy figure floats along.

Seek'st thou the plashy brink
Of weedy lake, or marge of river
    wide,
Or where the rocking billows rise
    and sink
    On the chafed ocean-side?

There is a Power whose care
Teaches thy way along that pathless
    coast—
The desert and illimitable air—
    Lone wandering, but not lost.

All day thy wings have fanned,
At that far height, the cold, thin
   atmosphere,
Yet stoop not, weary, to the wel-
   come land,
   Though the dark night is near.

And soon that toil shall end;
Soon shalt thou find a summer home,
   and rest,
And scream among thy fellows; reeds
   shall bend,
   Soon, o'er thy sheltered nest.

Thou'rt gone, the abyss of heaven
Hath swallowed up thy form; yet,
   on my heart
Deeply has sunk the lesson thou hast
   given,
   And shall not soon depart.

He who, from zone to zone,
Guides through the boundless sky
   thy certain flight,
In the long way that I must tread
   alone,
   Will lead my steps aright.

## INSCRIPTION FOR THE ENTRANCE TO A WOOD.

STRANGER, if thou hast learned a truth which needs
No school of long experience, that the world
Is full of guilt and misery, and hast seen
Enough of all its sorrows, crimes, and cares,
To tire thee of it, enter this wild wood
And view the haunts of Nature. The calm shade
Shall bring a kindred calm, and the sweet breeze
That makes the green leaves dance, shall waft a balm
To thy sick heart. Thou wilt find nothing here
Of all that pained thee in the haunts of men,
And made thee loathe thy life. The primal curse
Fell, it is true, upon the unsinning earth,

But not in vengeance. God hath
yoked to guilt
Her pale tormentor, misery. Hence,
these shades
Are still the abodes of gladness; the
thick roof
Of green and stirring branches is
alive
And musical with birds, that sing
and sport
In wantonness of spirit; while below
The squirrel, with raised paws and
form erect,
Chirps merrily. Throngs of insects
in the shade
Try their thin wings and dance in
the warm beam
That waked them into life. Even
the green trees
Partake the deep contentment; as
they bend
To the soft winds, the sun from the
blue sky
Looks in and sheds a blessing on the
scene.
Scarce less the cleft-born wild-flower
seems to enjoy
Existence than the wingèd plun-
derer

That sucks its sweets. The mossy
rocks themselves,
And the old and ponderous trunks of
prostrate trees
That lead from knoll to knoll a causey
rude
Or bridge the sunken brook, and their
dark roots,
With all their earth upon them, twist-
ing high,
Breathe fixed tranquillity. The rivu-
let
Sends forth glad sounds, and tripping
o'er its bed
Of pebbly sands, or leaping down the
rocks,
Seems, with continuous laughter, to
rejoice
In its own being. Softly tread the
marge,
Lest from her midway perch thou
scare the wren
That dips her bill in water. The
cool wind,
That stirs the stream in play, shall
come to thee,
Like one that loves thee nor will let
thee pass
Ungreeted, and shall give its light
embrace.

## THE WEST WIND.

Beneath the forest's skirt I rest,
Whose branching pines rise dark
and high,
And hear the breezes of the West
Among the thread-like foliage sigh.

Sweet Zephyr! why that sound of
woe?
Is not thy home among the flow-
ers?
Do not the bright June roses blow,
To meet thy kiss at morning hours?

And lo! thy glorious realm out-
spread—
Yon stretching valleys, green and
gay,
And yon free hill-tops, o'er whose
head
The loose white clouds are borne
away.

And there the full broad river runs,
And many a fount wells fresh and
sweet,

To cool thee when the mid-day suns
Have made thee faint beneath their
heat.

Thou wind of joy, and youth, and
love;
Spirit of the new-wakened year!
The sun in his blue realm above
Smooths a bright path when thou
art here.

In lawns the murmuring bee is heard,
The wooing ring-dove in the shade:
On thy soft breath, the new-fledged
bird
Takes wing, half happy, half
afraid.

Ah! thou art like our wayward
race;—
When not a shade of pain or ill
Dims the bright smile of Nature's
face,
Thou lov'st to sigh and murmur
still.

## OCTOBER.

Ay, thou art welcome, heaven's delicious breath!
  When woods begin to wear the crimson leaf,
    And suns grow meek, and the meek suns grow brief,
And the year smiles as it draws near its death.

Wind of the sunny south! oh, still delay
  In the gay woods and in the golden air,
  Like to a good old age released from care,
Journeying, in long serenity, away.
In such a bright, late quiet, would that I
  Might wear out life like thee, mid bowers and brooks,
  And, dearer yet, the sunshine of kind looks,
And music of kind voices ever nigh;
  And when my last sand twinkled in the glass,
  Pass silently from men, as thou dost pass.

-----

## NOVEMBER.

Yet one smile more, departing, distant sun!
  One mellow smile through the soft vapory air,
Ere, o'er the frozen earth, the loud winds run,
  Or snows are sifted o'er the meadows bare.
One smile on the brown hills and naked trees,
  And the dark rocks whose summer wreaths are cast,
And the blue gentian-flower, that, in the breeze,
  Nods lonely, of her beauteous race the last.
Yet a few sunny days, in which the bee
  Shall murmur by the hedge that skirts the way,
The cricket chirp upon the russet lea,
  And man delight to linger in thy ray.
Yet one rich smile, and we will try to bear
The piercing winter frost, and winds, and darkened air.

26

## A FOREST HYMN.

HE groves were God's first temples. Ere man learned
o hew the shaft, and lay the architrave,
nd spread the roof above them— ere he framed
he lofty vault, to gather and roll back
he sound of anthems; in the darkling wood,
.mid the cool and silence, he knelt down,
And offered to the Mightiest solemn thanks
And supplication. For his simple heart
Might not resist the sacred influence
Which, from the stilly twilight of the place,
And from the gray old trunks that high in heaven
Mingled their mossy boughs, and from the sound

Of the invisible breath that swayed at once
All their green tops, stole over him, and bowed
His spirit with the thought of boundless power
And inaccessible majesty. Ah, why
Should we, in the world's riper years, neglect
God's ancient sanctuaries, and adore
Only among the crowd, and under roofs
That our frail hands have raised? Let me, at least,
Here, in the shadow of this aged wood,
Offer one hymn—thrice happy, if it find
Acceptance in His ear.

Father, thy hand
Hath reared these venerable columns, thou
Didst weave this verdant roof. Thou didst look down
Upon the naked earth, and, forthwith, rose
All these fair ranks of trees. They, in thy sun,
Budded, and shook their green leaves in thy breeze,
And shot toward heaven. The century-living crow
Whose birth was in their tops, grew old and died
Among their branches, till, at last, they stood,
As now they stand, massy, and tall, and dark,
Fit shrine for humble worshipper to hold
Communion with his Maker. These dim vaults,
These winding aisles, of human pomp or pride

Report not. No fantastic carvings show
The boast of our vain race to change the form
Of thy fair works. But thou art here—thou fill'st
The solitude. Thou art in the soft winds
That run along the summit of these trees
In music; thou art in the cooler breath
That from the inmost darkness of the place
Comes, scarcely felt; the barky trunks, the ground,
The fresh moist ground, are all instinct with thee.
Here is continual worship;—Nature, here,
In the tranquillity that thou dost love,
Enjoys thy presence. Noiselessly, around,
From perch to perch, the solitary bird
Passes; and yon clear spring, that, midst its herbs,
Wells softly forth and wandering steeps the roots
Of half the mighty forest, tells no tale
Of all the good it does. Thou hast not left
Thyself without a witness, in the shades,
Of thy perfections. Grandeur, strength, and grace
Are here to speak of thee. This mighty oak—
By whose immovable stem I stand and seem
Almost annihilated—not a prince,
In all that proud old world beyond the deep,
E'er wore his crown as loftily as he

ears the green coronal of leaves with which
y hand has graced him. Nestled at his root

Is beauty, such as blooms not in the glare
Of the broad sun. That delicate forest flower,

ith scented breath and look so like a smile,
ems, as it issues from the shapeless mould,

An emanation of the indwelling Life,
A visible token of the upholding Love,
That are the soul of this great universe.

My heart is awed within me when
   I think
Of the great miracle that still goes on,
In silence, round me—the perpetual
   work
Of thy creation, finished, yet renewed
Forever. Written on thy works I read
The lesson of thy own eternity.
Lo! all grow old and die—but see
   again,
How on the faltering footsteps of decay
Youth presses—ever gay and beauti-
   ful youth
In all its beautiful forms. These
   lofty trees
Wave not less proudly that their
   ancestors
Moulder beneath them. Oh, there
   is not lost
One of earth's charms: upon her
   bosom yet,
After the flight of untold centuries,
The freshness of her far beginning lies
And yet shall lie. Life mocks the
   idle hate
Of his arch-enemy Death—yea, seats
   himself
Upon the tyrant's throne—the sepul-
   chre,
And of the triumphs of his ghastly foe
Makes his own nourishment. For he
   came forth
From thine own bosom, and shall
   have no end.

   There have been holy men who
   hid themselves
Deep in the woody wilderness, and
   gave
Their lives to thought and prayer,
*   till they outlived
The generation born with them, nor
   seemed

Less aged than the hoary trees and
   rocks
Around them;—and there have been
   holy men
Who deemed it were not well to pass
   life thus.
But let me often to these solitudes
Retire, and in thy presence reassure
My feeble virtue. Here its enemies,
The passions, at thy plainer footsteps
   shrink
And tremble and are still. O God!
   when thou
Dost scare the world with tempests,
   set on fire
The heavens with falling thunder-
   bolts, or fill,
With all the waters of the firmament,
The swift dark whirlwind that up-
   roots the woods
And drowns the villages; when, at
   thy call,
Uprises the great deep and throws
   himself
Upon the continent, and overwhelms
Its cities—who forgets not, at the sight
Of these tremendous tokens of thy
   power,
His pride, and lays his strifes and
   follies by?
Oh, from these sterner aspects of thy
   face
Spare me and mine, nor let us need
   the wrath
Of the mad unchained elements to
   teach
Who rules them. Be it ours to medi-
   tate,
In these calm shades, thy milder
   majesty,
And to the beautiful order of thy works
Learn to conform the order of our
   lives.

## THE FIRMAMENT.

Ay! gloriously thou standest there,
  Beautiful, boundless firmament!
That, swelling wide o'er earth and
    air,
  And round the horizon bent,
With thy bright vault, and sapphire
    wall,
Dost overhang and circle all.

Far, far below thee, tall gray trees
  Arise, and piles built up of old,

And hills, whose ancient summits
    freeze
  In the fierce light and cold.
The eagle soars his utmost height,
Yet far thou stretchest o'er his flight.

Thou hast thy frowns—with thee on
    high
  The storm has made his airy seat,
Beyond that soft blue curtain lie
  His stores of hail and sleet.

31

Thence the consuming lightnings
  break,
There the strong hurricanes awake.

Yet art thou prodigal of smiles—
  Smiles sweeter than thy frowns are
    stern.
Earth sends, from all her thousand
    isles,
  A shout at their return.
The glory that comes down from thee,
Bathes, in deep joy, the land and sea.

The sun, the gorgeous sun is thine,
  The pomp that brings and shuts the
    day,
The clouds that round him change
    and shine,
  The airs that fan his way.
Thence look the thoughtful stars, and
    there
The meek moon walks the silent air.

The sunny Italy may boast
  The beauteous tints that flush her
    skies,
And lovely, round the Grecian coast,
  May thy blue pillars rise.
I only know how fair they stand
Around my own beloved land.

And they are fair—a charm is theirs,
  That earth, the proud green earth,
    has not,
With all the forms, and hues, and airs,
  That haunt her sweetest spot.
We gaze upon thy calm pure sphere,
And read of Heaven's eternal year.

Oh, when, amid the throng of men,
  The heart grows sick of hollow
    mirth,
How willingly we turn us then
  Away from this cold earth,
And look into thy azure breast,
For seats of innocence and rest!

----

Think not that thou and I
Are here the only worshippers to-day,
  Beneath this glorious sky,
Mid the soft airs that o'er the meadows play;
  These airs, whose breathing stirs
The fresh grass, are our fellow-worshippers.

  See, as they pass, they swing
The censers of a thousand flowers that bend
  O'er the young herbs of spring,
And the sweet odors like a prayer ascend,
  While, passing thence, the breeze
Wakes the grave anthem of the forest-trees.

*From* Our Fellow-Worshippers.

## THE GLADNESS OF NATURE.

Is this a time to be cloudy and sad,
  When our mother Nature laughs
    around;
When even the deep blue heavens
  look glad,
  And gladness breathes from the
    blossoming ground?

There are notes of joy from the hang-
  bird and wren,
  And the gossip of swallows through
    all the sky;

The ground-squirrel gayly chirps by
  his den.
  And the wilding bee hums merrily
    by.

The clouds are at play in the azure
  space
  And their shadows at play on the
    bright-green vale,
And here they stretch to the frolic
  chase,
  And there they roll on the easy gale.

There's a dance of leaves in that
   aspen bower,
  There's a titter of winds in that
   beechen tree,
There's a smile on the fruit, and a
   smile on the flower,
  And a laugh from the brook that
   runs to the sea.

And look at the broad-faced sun,
   how he smiles
  On the dewy earth that smiles in
   his ray,
On the leaping waters and gay young
   isles;
  Ay, look, and he'll smile thy gloom
   away.

### "I BROKE THE SPELL THAT HELD ME LONG."

I BROKE the spell that held me long,
The dear, dear witchery of song.
I said, the poet's idle lore
Shall waste my prime of years no
   more,
For Poetry, though heavenly born,
Consorts with poverty and scorn.

I broke the spell — nor deemed its
   power
Could fetter me another hour.
Ah, thoughtless! how could I forget

Its causes were around me yet?
For wheresoe'er I looked, the while,
Was Nature's everlasting smile.

Still came and lingered on my sight
Of flowers and streams the bloom
   and light,
And glory of the stars and sun;—
And these and poetry are one.
They, ere the world had held me
   long,
Recalled me to the love of song.

## MIDSUMMER.

A POWER is on the earth and in the air
  From which the vital spirit shrinks afraid,
  And shelters him, in nooks of deepest shade,
From the hot steam and from the fiery glare.
Look forth upon the earth—her thousand plants
  Are smitten; even the dark sun-loving maize
  Faints in the field beneath the torrid blaze;

The herd beside the shaded fountain pants;
For life is driven from all the landscape brown;
  The bird has sought his tree, the snake his den,
  The trout floats dead in the hot stream, and men
Drop by the sun-stroke in the populous town;
  As if the Day of Fire had dawned, and sent
  Its deadly breath into the firmament.

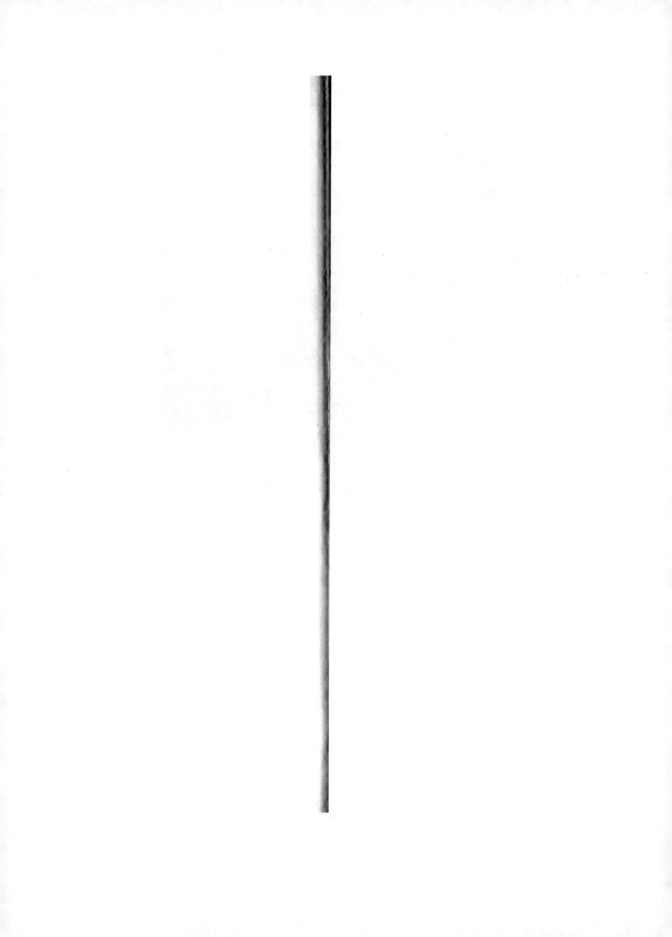

## WILLIAM TELL.

CHAINS may subdue the feeble spirit,
  but thee,
  TELL, of the iron heart! they could
  not tame!
  For thou wert of the mountains;
  they proclaim
The everlasting creed of liberty.
That creed is written on the un-
  trampled snow,
  Thundered by torrents which no
  power can hold,
  Save that of God, when He sends
  forth His cold,

And breathed by winds that through
  the free heaven blow.
Thou, while thy prison-walls were
  dark around,
  Didst meditate the lesson Nature
  taught,
  And to thy brief captivity was
  brought
A vision of thy Switzerland unbound.
  The bitter cup they mingled,
  strengthened thee
  For the great work to set thy
  country free.

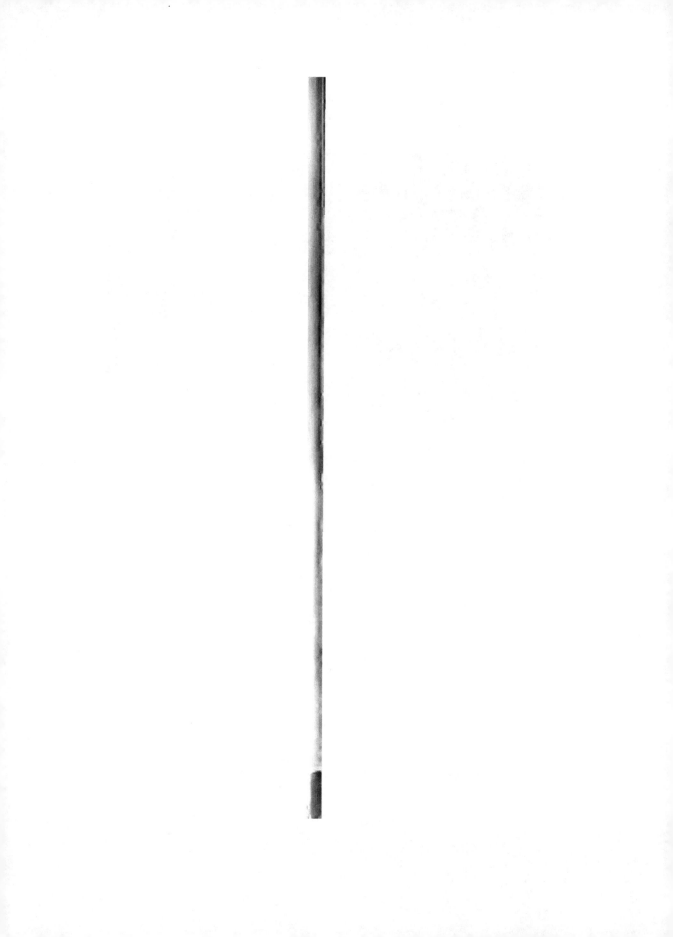

## TO THE FRINGED GENTIAN.

Thou blossom bright with autumn
dew,
And colored with the heaven's own
blue,
That openest when the quiet light
Succeeds the keen and frosty night.

Thou comest not when violets lean
O'er wandering brooks and springs
unseen,
Or columbines, in purple dressed,
Nod o'er the ground-bird's hidden
nest.

Thou waitest late and com'st alone,
When woods are bare and birds are
flown,
And frosts and shortening days por-
tend
The aged year is near his end.

Then doth thy sweet and quiet eye
Look through its fringes to the sky,
Blue — blue — as if that sky let
fall
A flower from its cerulean wall.

I would that thus, when I shall
see
The hour of death draw near to
me,
Hope, blossoming within my heart,
May look to heaven as I depart.

## "INNOCENT CHILD AND SNOW-WHITE FLOWER."

INNOCENT child and snow - white
flower!
Well are ye paired in your opening
hour.
Thus should the pure and the lovely
meet,
Stainless with stainless, and sweet
with sweet.

White as those leaves, just blown
apart,
Are the folds of thy own young
heart;

Guilty passion and cankering care
Never have left their traces there.

Artless one! though thou gazest now
O'er the white blossom with earnest
brow,
Soon will it tire thy childish eye;
Fair as it is, thou wilt throw it by.

Throw it aside in thy weary hour,
Throw to the ground the fair white
flower;
Yet, as thy tender years depart,
Keep that white and innocent heart.

41

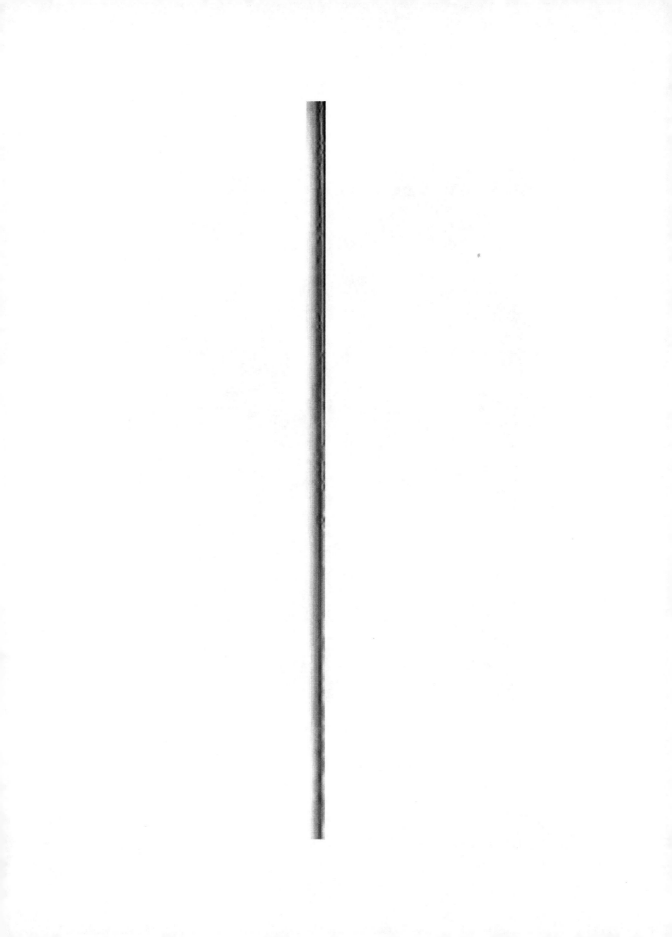

## THE TWENTY-SECOND OF DECEMBER.

Vɪʟᴅ was the day; the wintry sea
Moaned sadly on New-England's
strand,

When first the thoughtful and the
free,
Our fathers, trod the desert land.

43

They little thought how pure a light,
　With years, should gather round
　　that day;
How love should keep their memories
　bright,
　How wide a realm their sons should
　　sway.

Green are their bays; but greener still
　Shall round their spreading fame
　　be wreathed,

And　regions,　now　untrod,　shall
　thrill　　　　　.
　With reverence when their names
　　are breathed.

Till　where　the　sun,　with　softer
　fires,
　Looks on the vast Pacific's sleep,
The children of the pilgrim sires
　This　hallowed　day　like　us　shall
　　keep.

---

## "THOU, GOD, SEEST ME."

When this song of praise shall cease,
　Let thy children, Lord, depart
With the blessing of thy peace
　And thy love in every heart.

Oh, where'er our path may lie,
　Father, let us not forget
That we walk beneath thine eye,
　That thy care upholds us yet.

Blind are we, and weak, and frail;
　Be thine aid forever near;
May the fear to sin prevail
　Over every other fear.

44

## SEVENTY-SIX.

WHAT heroes from the woodland sprung,
  When, through the fresh-awakened land,
The thrilling cry of freedom rung
And to the work of warfare strung
  The yeoman's iron hand!

Hills flung the cry to hills around,
  And ocean - mart replied to mart,
And streams, whose springs were yet unfound,
Pealed far away the startling sound
  Into the forest's heart.

Then marched the brave from rocky
    steep,
  From mountain-river swift and cold;
The borders of the stormy deep,
The vales where gathered waters sleep,
  Sent up the strong and bold,—

As if the very earth again
  Grew quick with God's creating
    breath,
And, from the sods of grove and glen,
Rose ranks of lion-hearted men
  To battle to the death.

The wife, whose babe first smiled
    that day,
  The fair fond bride of yestereve,

And aged sire and matron gray,
Saw the loved warriors haste away,
  And deemed it sin to grieve.

Already had the strife begun;
  Already blood, on Concord's plain,
Along the springing grass had run,
And blood had flowed at Lexington,
  Like brooks of April rain.

That death - stain on the vernal
    sward
  Hallowed to freedom all the
    shore;
In fragments fell the yoke abhorred—
The footstep of a foreign lord
  Profaned the soil no more.

---

## THE BATTLE OF BENNINGTON.

On this fair valley's grassy breast
The calm, sweet rays of summer rest,
And dove-like peace divinely broods
On its smooth lawns and solemn
    woods.

A century since, in flame and smoke,
The storm of battle o'er it broke;
And ere the invader turned and fled,
These pleasant fields were strown
    with dead.

Stark, quick to act and bold to dare,
And Warner's mountain band were
    there;
And Allen, who had flung the pen
Aside to lead the Berkshire men.

With fiery onset—blow on blow—
They rushed upon the embattled foe,

And swept his squadrons from the
    vale,
Like leaves before the autumn gale.

Oh! never may the purple stain
Of combat blot these fields again,
Nor this fair valley ever cease
To wear the placid smile of peace.

But we, beside this battle-field,
Will plight the vow that ere we yield
The right for which our fathers bled,
Our blood shall steep the ground we
    tread.

And men shall hold the memory dear
Of those who fought for freedom
    here,
And guard the heritage they won
While these green hill-sides feel the
    sun.

## THE ANTIQUITY OF FREEDOM.

HERE are old trees, tall oaks, and gnarlèd pines,
That stream with gray-green mosses; here the ground
Was never trenched by spade, and flowers spring up
Unsown, and die ungathered. It is sweet

To linger here, among the flitting birds
And leaping squirrels, wandering
    brooks, and winds
That shake the leaves, and scatter,
    as they pass,
A fragrance from the cedars, thickly
    set
With pale-blue berries. In these
    peaceful shades—
Peaceful, unpruned, immeasurably
    old—
My thoughts go up the long dim
    path of years,
Back to the earliest days of liberty.

O FREEDOM! thou art not, as poets
    dream,
A fair young girl, with light and
    delicate limbs,
And wavy tresses gushing from the
    cap
With which the Roman master
    crowned his slave
When he took off the gyves. A
    bearded man,
Armed to the teeth, art thou; one
    mailèd hand
Grasps the broad shield, and one the
    sword; thy brow,
Glorious in beauty though it be, is
    scarred
With tokens of old wars; thy massive
    limbs
Are strong with struggling. Power
    at thee has launched
His bolts, and with his lightnings
    smitten thee;
They could not quench the life thou
    hast from heaven;
Merciless Power has dug thy dungeon
    deep,
And his swart armorers, by a thou-
    sand fires,

Have forged thy chain; yet, while he
    deems thee bound,
The links are shivered, and the
    prison-walls
Fall outward; terribly thou springest
    forth,
As springs the flame above a burning
    pile,
And shoutest to the nations, who
    return
Thy shoutings, while the pale op-
    pressor flies.

Thy birthright was not given by
    human hands:
Thou wert twin-born with man. In
    pleasant fields,
While yet our race was few, thou
    sat'st with him,
To tend the quiet flock and watch
    the stars,
And teach the reed to utter simple
    airs.
Thou by his side, amid the tangled
    wood,
Didst war upon the panther and the
    wolf,
His only foes; and thou with him
    didst draw
The earliest furrow on the mountain-
    side,
Soft with the deluge. Tyranny him-
    self,
Thy enemy, although of reverend
    look,
Hoary with many years, and far
    obeyed,
Is later born than thou; and as he
    meets
The grave defiance of thine elder
    eye,
The usurper trembles in his fast-
    nesses.

Thou shalt wax stronger with the lapse of years,
But he shall fade into a feebler age—
Feebler, yet subtler. He shall weave his snares,

And spring them on thy careless steps, and clap
His withered hands, and from their ambush call
His hordes to fall upon thee. He shall send

Quaint maskers, wearing fair and gallant forms
To catch thy gaze, and uttering graceful words
To charm thy ear; while his sly imps by stealth,
Twine round thee threads of steel, light thread on thread,

That grow to fetters; or bind down thy arms
With chains concealed in chaplets. Oh! not yet
Mayst thou unbrace thy corslet, nor lay by
Thy sword; nor yet, O Freedom! close thy lids

In slumber; for thine enemy never
  sleeps,
And thou must watch and combat
  till the day
Of the new earth and heaven. But
  wouldst thou rest
Awhile from tumult and the frauds
  of men,

These old and friendly solitudes invite
Thy visit. They, while yet the for-
  est-trees
Were young upon the unviolated earth,
And yet the moss-stains on the rock
  were new,
Beheld thy glorious childhood, and
  rejoiced.

50

## THE WHITE-FOOTED DEER.

It was a hundred years ago,
  When, by the woodland ways,
The traveller saw the wild - deer
    drink,
  Or crop the birchen sprays.

Beneath a hill, whose rocky side
  O'erbrowed a grassy mead,
And fenced a cottage from the
    wind,
  A deer was wont to feed.

She only came when on the cliffs
  The evening moonlight lay,

And no man knew the secret haunts
  In which she walked by day.

White were her feet, her forehead
    showed
  A spot of silvery white,
That seemed to glimmer like a star
  In autumn's hazy night.

And here, when sang the whippoorwill,
  She cropped the sprouting leaves,
And here her rustling steps were
    heard
  On still October eves.

51

But when the broad midsummer moon
 Rose o'er that grassy lawn,
Beside the silver-footed deer
 There grazed a spotted fawn.

The cottage dame forbade her son
 To aim the rifle here;
"It were a sin," she said, "to harm
 Or fright that friendly deer.

"This spot has been my pleasant home
 Ten peaceful years and more;
And ever, when the moonlight shines,
 She feeds before our door.

"The red-men say that here she
  walked
 A thousand moons ago;
They never raise the war-whoop
  here,
 And never twang the bow.

"I love to watch her as she feeds,
 And think that all is well
While such a gentle creature haunts
 The place in which we dwell."

The youth obeyed, and sought for
  game
 In forests far away,
Where, deep in silence and in moss,
 The ancient woodland lay.

But once, in autumn's golden time
 He ranged the wild in vain,

Nor roused the pheasant nor the deer,
 And wandered home again.

The crescent moon and crimson eve
 Shone with a mingling light;
The deer, upon the grassy mead,
 Was feeding full in sight.

He raised the rifle to his eye,
 And from the cliffs around
A sudden echo, shrill and sharp,
 Gave back its deadly sound.

Away, into the neighboring wood,
 The startled creature flew,
And crimson drops at morning lay
 Amid the glimmering dew.

Next evening shone the waxing
  moon
 As brightly as before;
The deer upon the grassy mead
 Was seen again no more.

But ere that crescent moon was
  old,
 By night the red-men came,
And burnt the cottage to the ground,
 And slew the youth and dame.

Now woods have overgrown the
  mead,
 And hid the cliffs from sight;
There shrieks the hovering hawk at
  noon,
 And prowls the fox at night.

## THE LAND OF DREAMS.

A MIGHTY realm is the Land of
 Dreams,
  With steeps that hang in the twi-
   light sky,
And weltering oceans and trailing
 streams,
  That gleam where the dusky valleys
   lie.

But over its shadowy border flow
  Sweet rays from the world of end-
   less morn,

And the nearer mountains catch the
 glow,
  And flowers in the nearer fields
   are born.

The souls of the happy dead repair,
  From their bowers of light, to that
   bordering land,
And walk in the fainter glory
 there,
  With the souls of the living hand
   in hand.

53

One calm sweet smile, in that shadowy sphere,
 From eyes that open on earth no
  more—
One warning word from a voice once
 dear—
 How they rise in the memory o'er
  and o'er!

Far off from those hills that shine
 with day
 And fields that bloom in the
  heavenly gales,
The Land of Dreams goes stretching
 away
 To dimmer mountains and darker
  vales.

There lie the chambers of guilty delight,
 There walk the specters of guilty
  fear,
And soft low voices, that float
 through the night,
 Are whispering sin in the helpless
  ear.

Dear maid, in thy girlhood's opening
 flower,
 Scarce weaned from the love of
  childish play!

The tears on whose cheeks are but
 the shower
 That freshens the blooms of early
  May!

Thine eyes are closed, and over thy
 brow
 Pass thoughtful shadows and joy-
  ous gleams,
And I know, by thy moving lips, that
 now
 Thy spirit strays in the Land of
  Dreams.

Light-hearted maiden, oh, heed thy
 feet!
 O keep where that beam of Paradise falls:
And only wander where thou mayst
 meet
 The blessed ones from its shining
  walls!

So shalt thou come from the Land of
 Dreams,
 With love and peace to this world
  of strife:
And the light which over that border
 streams
 Shall lie on the path of thy daily
  life.

## THE PLANTING OF THE APPLE-TREE.

COME, let us plant the apple-tree.
Cleave the tough greensward with
    the spade;
Wide let its hollow bed be made;
There gently lay the roots, and there
Sift the dark mould with kindly
    care,
    And press it o'er them tenderly,
As, round the sleeping infant's feet,
We softly fold the cradle-sheet;
    So plant we the apple-tree.

    What plant we in this apple-tree?
Buds, which the breath of summer
    days
Shall lengthen into leafy sprays;
Boughs where the thrush, with crim-
    son breast,
Shall haunt and sing and hide her
    nest;

We plant, upon the sunny lea,
A shadow for the noontide hour,
A shelter from the summer shower,
    When we plant the apple-tree.

    What plant we in this apple-tree?
Sweets for a hundred flowery springs
To load the May-wind's restless
    wings,
When, from the orchard-row, he
    pours
Its fragrance through our open doors;
    A world of blossoms for the bee,
Flowers for the sick girl's silent room,
For the glad infant sprigs of bloom,
    We plant with the apple-tree.

    What plant we in this apple-tree?
Fruits that shall swell in sunny June,
And redden in the August noon,

55

And drop, when gentle airs come by,
That fan the blue September sky,
  While children come, with cries of
    glee,
And seek them where the fragrant
  grass
Betrays their bed to those who pass,
  At the foot of the apple-tree.

And when, above this apple-tree,
The winter stars are quivering bright,
And winds go howling through the
  night,
Girls, whose young eyes o'erflow
  with mirth,
Shall peel its fruit by cottage-
  hearth,
  And guests in prouder homes shall
    see,
Heaped with the grape of Cintra's
  vine
And golden orange of the line,
  The fruit of the apple-tree.

The fruitage of this apple-tree
Winds and our flag of stripe and star
Shall bear to coasts that lie afar,
Where men shall wonder at the
  view,
And ask in what fair groves they
  grew;
  And sojourners beyond the sea
Shall think of childhood's careless day,
And long, long hours of summer
  play,
  In the shade of the apple-tree.

Each year shall give this apple-tree
A broader flush of roseate bloom,
A deeper maze of verdurous gloom,
And loosen, when the frost-clouds
  lower,
The crisp brown leaves in thicker
  shower.
  The years shall come and pass, but
    we
Shall hear no longer, where we lie,
The summer's songs, the autumn's sigh,
  In the boughs of the apple-tree.

And time shall waste this apple-tree.
Oh, when its aged branches throw
Thin shadows on the ground below,
Shall fraud and force and iron will
Oppress the weak and helpless still?
  What shall the tasks of mercy be,
Amid the toils, the strifes, the tears
Of those who live when length of
  years
  Is wasting this little apple-tree?

"Who planted this old apple-
  tree?"
The children of that distant day
Thus to some aged man shall say;
And, gazing on its mossy stem,
The gray-haired man shall answer
  them:
"A poet of the land was he,
Born in the rude but good old times;
'Tis said he made some quaint old
  rhymes,
  On planting the apple-tree."

## THE SNOW-SHOWER.

STAND here by my side and turn, I
    pray,
  On the lake below, thy gentle
    eyes;

The clouds hang over it, heavy and
    gray,
  And dark and silent the water
    lies;

57

And out of that frozen mist the snow
In wavering flakes begins to flow;
   Flake after flake
They sink in the dark and silent lake.
See how in a living swarm they
  come
 From the chambers beyond that
  misty veil;
Some hover awhile in air, and some
 Rush prone from the sky like sum-
  mer hail.
All, dropping swiftly or settling slow,
Meet, and are still in the depths be-
  low;
   Flake after flake
Dissolved in the dark and silent lake.
Here delicate snow-stars, out of the
  cloud,
 Come floating downward in airy
  play,
Like spangles dropped from the
  glistening crowd
 That whiten by night the milky
  way;
There broader and burlier masses
  fall;
The sullen water buries them all—
   Flake after flake—
All drowned in the dark and silent
  lake.

And some, as on tender wings they
  glide
 From their chilly birth-cloud, dim
  and gray,
Are joined in their fall, and, side by
  side,
 Come clinging along their unsteady
  way;
As friend with friend, or husband
  with wife,
Makes hand in hand the passage of
  life;

   Each mated flake
Soon sinks in the dark and silent
  lake.

Lo! while we are gazing, in swifter
  haste
 Stream down the snows, till the
  air is white,
As, myriads by myriads madly chased,
 They fling themselves from their
  shadowy height.
The fair, frail creatures of middle
  sky,
What speed they make, with their
  graves so nigh;
   Flake after flake,
To lie in the dark and silent lake!

I see in thy gentle eyes a tear;
 They turn to me in sorrowful
  thought;
Thou thinkest of friends, the good
  and dear,
 Who were for a time, and now are
  not;
Like these fair children of cloud and
  frost,
That glisten a moment and then are
  lost,
   Flake after flake—
All lost in the dark and silent lake.

Yet look again, for the clouds divide;
 A gleam of blue on the water lies;
And far away, on the mountain-side,
 A sunbeam falls from the opening
  skies,
But the hurrying host that flew be-
  tween
The cloud and the water, no more is
  seen;
   Flake after flake,
At rest in the dark and silent lake.

## ROBERT OF LINCOLN.

Merrily swinging on brier and weed,
  Near to the nest of his little dame,
Over the mountain-side or mead,
  Robert of Lincoln is telling his
    name:
      Bob-o'-link, bob-o'-link,
      Spink, spank, spink;

Snug and safe is that nest of ours,
Hidden among the summer flowers.
      Chee, chee, chee.

Robert of Lincoln is gayly drest,
  Wearing a bright black wedding-
    coat;

59

White are his shoulders and white
　his crest.
　Hear him call in his merry note:
　　Bob-o'-link, bob-o'-link,
　　Spink, spank, spink;
Look, what a nice new coat is mine,
Sure there was never a bird so fine.
　　　　Chee, chee, chee.

Robert of Lincoln's Quaker wife,
　Pretty and quiet, with plain brown
　　wings,
Passing at home a patient life,
　Broods in the grass while her hus-
　　band sings:
　　Bob-o'-link, bob-o'-link,
　　Spink, spank, spink;
Brood, kind creature; you need not
　fear
Thieves and robbers while I am here.
　　　　Chee, chee, chee.

Modest and shy as a nun is she;
　One weak chirp is her only note.
Braggart and prince of braggarts is
　he,
　Pouring boasts from his little
　　throat:
　　Bob-o'-link, bob-o'-link,
　　Spink, spank, spink;
Never was I afraid of man;
Catch me, cowardly knaves, if you
　can!
　　　　Chee, chee, chee.

Six white eggs on a bed of hay,
　Flecked with purple, a pretty sight!
There as the mother sits all day,
　Robert is singing with all his might:

　　Bob-o'-link, bob-o'-link,
　　Spink, spank, spink;
Nice good wife, that never goes out,
Keeping house while I frolic about.
　　　　Chee, chee, chee.

Soon as the little ones chip the shell,
　Six wide mouths are open for food;
Robert of Lincoln bestirs him well,
　Gathering seeds for the hungry
　　brood.
　　Bob-o'-link, bob-o'-link,
　　Spink, spank, spink;
This new life is likely to be
Hard for a gay young fellow like me.
　　　　Chee, chee, chee.

Robert of Lincoln at length is made
　Sober with work, and silent with
　　care;
Off is his holiday garment laid,
　Half forgotten that merry air:
　　Bob-o' link, bob-o'-link,
　　Spink, spank, spink;
Nobody knows but my mate and I
Where our nest and our nestlings lie.
　　　　Chee, chee, chee.

Summer wanes; the children are
　　grown;
　Fun and frolic no more he knows;
Robert of Lincoln's a humdrum crone;
　Off he flies, and we sing as he goes:
　　Bob-o'-link, bob-o'-link,
　　Spink, spank, spink;
When you can pipe that merry old
　strain,
Robert of Lincoln, come back again.
　　　　Chee, chee, chee.

60

## A SONG FOR NEW-YEAR'S EVE.

Stay yet, my friends, a moment stay—
  Stay till the good old year,
So long companion of our way,
  Shakes hands, and leaves us here.
      Oh stay, oh stay,
One little hour, and then away.

The year, whose hopes were high
    and strong,
  Has now no hopes to wake;
Yet one hour more of jest and song
  For his familiar sake.
      Oh stay, oh stay,
One mirthful hour, and then away.

The kindly year, his liberal hands
  Have lavished all his store.
And shall we turn from where he
    stands,
  Because he gives no more?
      Oh stay, oh stay,
One grateful hour, and then away.

Days brightly came and calmly went,
  While yet he was our guest;
How cheerfully the week was spent!
  How sweet the seventh day's rest!
      Oh stay, oh stay,
One golden hour, and then away.

Dear friends were with us, some who
    sleep
  Beneath the coffin-lid:
What pleasant memories we keep
  Of all they said and did!
      Oh stay, oh stay,
One tender hour, and then away.

Even while we sing, he smiles his
    last,
  And leaves our sphere behind.
The good old year is with the past;
  Oh be the new as kind!
      Oh stay, oh stay,
One parting strain, and then away.

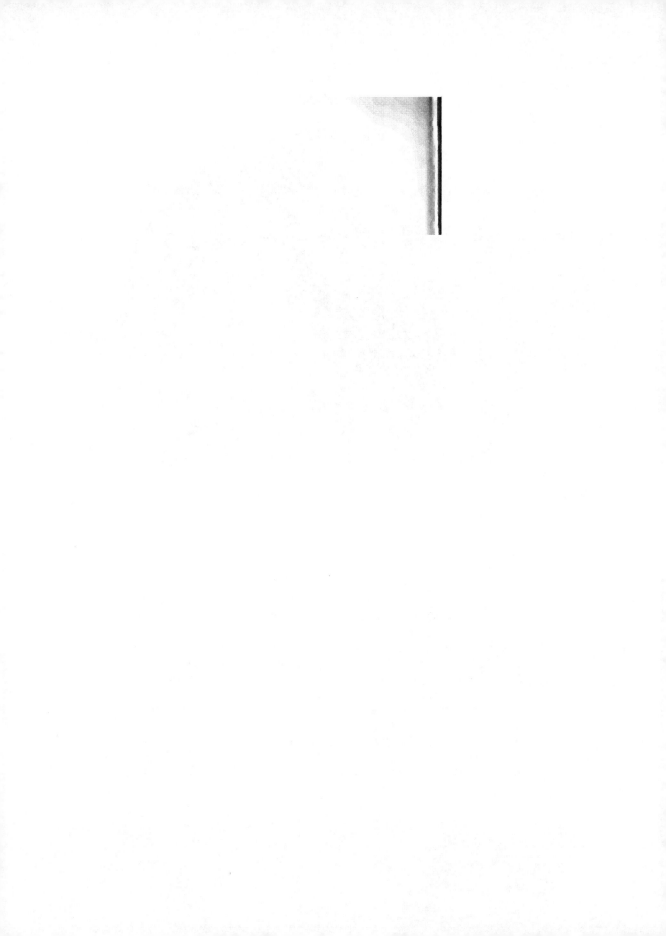

## THE LITTLE PEOPLE OF THE SNOW.

*Alice.*—One of your old-world stories, Uncle John,
Such as you tell us by the winter fire,
Till we all wonder it is grown so late.
*Uncle John.*—The story of the witch that ground to death
Two children in her mill, or will you have
The tale of Goody Cutpurse?
*Alice.*—        Nay now, nay;
Those stories are too childish, Uncle John,
Too childish even for little Willy here,
And I am older, two good years, than he;
No, let us have a tale of elves that ride,
By night, with jingling reins, or gnomes of the mine,
Or water-fairies, such as you know how
To spin, till Willy's eyes forget to wink,
And good Aunt Mary, busy as she is,
Lays down her knitting.
*Uncle John.*—        Listen to me, then.
'Twas in the olden time, long, long ago,
And long before the great oak at our door
Was yet an acorn, on a mountain's side
Lived, with his wife, a cottager. They dwelt

Beside a glen and near a dashing brook,
A pleasant spot in spring, where first the wren
Was heard to chatter, and, among the grass,
Flowers opened earliest; but when winter came,
That little brook was fringed with other flowers,—
White flowers, with crystal leaf and stem, that grew

In clear November nights. And, later still,
That mountain-glen was filled with drifted snows
From side to side, that one might walk across;
While, many a fathom deep, below, the brook
Sang to itself, and leaped and trotted on
Unfrozen, o'er its pebbles, toward the vale.

*Alice.*—A mountain-side, you said; the Alps, perhaps,
Or our own Alleghanies.
   *Uncle John.*—    Not so fast,

My young geographer, for then the Alps,
With their broad pastures, haply were untrod

Of herdsman's foot, and never human
voice
Had sounded in the woods that overhang

Our Alleghany's streams.    I think it
was
Upon the slopes of the great Caucasus,
Or where the rivulets of Ararat

Seek the Armenian vales.    That
mountain rose
So high, that, on its top, the winter-
snow
Was never melted, and the cottagers
Among the summer-blossoms, far be-
low,
Saw its white peaks in August from
their door.
   One little maiden, in that cottage-
home,
Dwelt with her parents, light of heart
and limb,
Bright, restless, thoughtless, flitting
here and there,
Like sunshine on the uneasy ocean-
waves,
And sometimes she forgot what she
was bid,
As Alice does.
   *Alice.*—    Or Willy, quite as oft.
   *Uncle John.*—But you are older,
Alice, two good years,
And should be wiser.  Eva was the
name
Of this young maiden, now twelve
summers old.

Now you must know that, in those
early times,
When autumn days grew pale, there
came a troop
Of childlike forms from that cold
mountain-top;
With trailing garments through the
air they came,
Or walked the ground with girded
loins, and threw
Spangles of silvery frost upon the grass,
And edged the brooks with glistening
parapets,
And built it crystal bridges, touched
the pool,
And turned its face to glass, or, rising
thence,
They shook from their full laps the
soft, light snow,
And buried the great earth, as
autumn winds
Bury the forest - floor in heaps of
leaves.
   A beautiful race were they, with
baby brows,
And fair, bright locks, and voices
like the sound

Of steps on the crisp snow, in which
    they talked
With man, as friend with friend. A
    merry sight
It was, when, crowding round the
    traveller,

They smote him with their heaviest
    snow-flakes, flung
Needles of frost in handfuls at his
    cheeks,
And, of the light wreaths of his
    smoking breath,

Wove a white fringe for his brown
    beard, and laughed
Their slender laugh to see him wink
    and grin
And make grim faces as he floundered
    on.
    But, when the spring came on,
    what terror reigned

Among these Little People of the
    Snow!
To them the sun's warm beams were
    shafts of fire,
And the soft south-wind was the
    wind of death.
Away they flew, all with a pretty
    scowl

Upon their childish faces, to the north,
Or scampered upward to the mountain's top,
And there defied their enemy, the Spring;
Skipping and dancing on the frozen peaks,
And moulding little snow-balls in their palms,
And rolling them, to crush her flowers below,
Down the steep snow-fields.

*Alice.*— That, too, must have been A merry sight to look at.

*Uncle John.*—        You are right,

But I must speak of graver matters now.
Midwinter was the time, and Eva stood,
Within the cottage, all prepared to dare
The outer cold, with ample furry robe
Close-belted round her waist, and boots of fur,
And a broad kerchief, which her mother's hand
Had closely drawn about her ruddy cheek.
"Now, stay not long abroad," said the good dame,
"For sharp is the outer air, and, mark me well,
Go not upon the snow beyond the spot

Where the great linden bounds the
neighboring field."
The little maiden promised, and
went forth,
And climbed the rounded snow-swells
firm with frost
Beneath her feet, and slid, with bal-
ancing arms,
Into the hollows. Once, as up a drift
She slowly rose, before her, in the
way,
She saw a little creature, lily-cheeked,
With flowing flaxen locks, and faint
blue eyes,
That gleamed like ice, and robe that
only seemed
Of a more shadowy whiteness than
her cheek.
On a smooth bank she sat.
  *Alice.—*          She must have been
One of your Little People of the
Snow.
  *Uncle John.—*She was so, and, as
Eva now drew near,
The tiny creature bounded from her
seat;
"And come," she said, "my pretty
friend; to-day
We will be playmates. I have
watched thee long,
And seen how well thou lov'st to
walk these drifts,
And scoop their fair sides into little
cells,
And carve them with quaint figures,
huge-limbed men,
Lions, and griffins. We will have,
to-day,
A merry ramble over these bright
fields,
And thou shalt see what thou hast
never seen."
On went the pair, until they reached
the bound

Where the great linden stood, set
deep in snow,
Up to the lower branches. "Here
we stop,"
Said Eva, "for my mother has my
word
That I will go no farther than this
tree."
Then the snow - maiden laughed:
"And what is this?
This fear of the pure snow, the
innocent snow,
That never harmed aught living?
Thou mayst roam
For leagues beyond this garden, and
return
In safety; here the grim wolf never
prowls,
And here the eagle of our mountain-
crags
Preys not in winter. I will show
the way,
And bring thee safely home. Thy
mother, sure,
Counselled thee thus because thou
hadst no guide."
  By such smooth words was Eva
won to break
Her promise, and went on with her
new friend,
Over the glistening snow and down a
bank
Where a white shelf, wrought by the
eddying wind,
Like to a billow's crest in the great
sea,
Curtained an opening. "Look, we
enter here."
And straight, beneath the fair o'er-
hanging fold,
Entered the little pair that hill of
snow,
Walking along a passage with white
walls,

And a white vault above where snow-stars shed
A wintry twilight. Eva moved in awe,

And held her peace, but the snow-maiden smiled,
And talked and tripped along, as, down the way,

Deeper they went into that mountainous drift.
And now the white walls widened, and the vault
Swelled upward, like some vast cathedral-dome,

Such as the Florentine, who bore the name
Of heaven's most potent angel, reared, long since,
Or the unknown builder of that wondrous fane,

The glory of Burgos. Here a garden
lay,
In which the Little People of the Snow
Were wont to take their pastime
when their tasks
Upon the mountain's side and in the
clouds
Were ended. Here they taught the
silent frost
To mock, in stem and spray, and leaf
and flower,
The growths of summer. Here the
palm upreared
Its white columnar trunk and spotless
sheaf
Of plume - like leaves; here cedars,
huge as those
Of Lebanon, stretched far their level
boughs,
Yet pale and shadowless; the sturdy
oak
Stood, with its huge gnarled roots of
seeming strength,
Fast anchored in the glistening bank;
light sprays
Of myrtle, roses in their bud and
bloom,
Drooped by the winding walks; yet
all seemed wrought
Of stainless alabaster; up the trees
Ran the lithe jessamine, with stalk
and leaf
Colorless as her flowers. "Go softly
on,"
Said the snow-maiden; "touch not,
with thy hand,
The frail creation round thee, and
beware
To sweep it with thy skirts. Now
look above.
How sumptuously these bowers are
lighted up
With shifting gleams that softly come
and go!

These are the northern lights, such
as thou seest
In the midwinter nights, cold, wandering flames,
That float with our processions,
through the air;
And here, within our winter palaces,
Mimic the glorious daybreak." Then
she told
How, when the wind, in the long
winter nights,
Swept the light snows into the hollow
dell,
She and her comrades guided to its
place
Each wandering flake, and piled them
quaintly up,
In shapely colonnade and glistening
arch,
With shadowy aisles between, or
bade them grow,
Beneath their little hands, to bowery
walks
In gardens such as these, and, o'er
them all,
Built the broad roof. "But thou
hast yet to see
A fairer sight," she said, and led the
way
To where a window of pellucid ice
Stood in the wall of snow, beside
their path.
"Look, but thou mayst not enter."
Eva looked,
And lo! a glorious hall, from whose
high vault
Stripes of soft light, ruddy and
delicate green,
And tender blue, flowed downward
to the floor
And far around, as if the aërial
hosts,
That march on high by night, with
beamy spears,

70

And streaming banners, to that place had brought
Their radiant flags to grace a festival.
    And in that hall a joyous multitude
Of those by whom its glistening walls were reared,
Whirled in a merry dance to silvery sounds,
That rang from cymbals of transparent ice,
And ice-cups, quivering to the skilful touch

Of little fingers.  Round and round they flew,
As when, in spring, about a chimney-top,
A cloud of twittering swallows, just returned,
Wheel round and round, and turn and wheel again,
Unwinding their swift track.  So rapidly
Flowed the meandering stream of that fair dance,
Beneath that dome of light.  Bright eyes that looked
From under lily-brows, and gauzy scarfs
Sparkling like snow-wreaths in the early sun,
Shot by the window in their mazy whirl.

And there stood Eva, wondering at the sight
Of those bright revellers and that graceful sweep
Of motion as they passed her;—long she gazed,
And listened long to the sweet sounds that thrilled
The frosty air, till now the encroaching cold
Recalled her to herself.  "Too long, too long
I linger here," she said, and then she sprang
Into the path, and with a hurried step
Followed it upward.  Ever by her side
Her little guide kept pace.  As on they went,

Eva bemoaned her fault: "What must they think—
The dear ones in the cottage, while so long,
Hour after hour, I stay without? I know
That they will seek me far and near, and weep

To find me not. How could I, wickedly,
Neglect the charge they gave me?" As she spoke,
The hot tears started to her eyes; she knelt
In the mid-path. "Father! forgive this sin;

Forgive myself I cannot "—thus she prayed,
And rose and hastened onward. When, at last,
They reached the outer air, the clear north breathed
A bitter cold, from which she shrank with dread,

But the snow-maiden bounded as she felt
The cutting blast, and uttered shouts of joy,
And skipped, with boundless glee, from drift to drift,
And danced round Eva, as she labored up

The mounds of snow. "Ah me! I feel my eyes
Grow heavy," Eva said; "they swim with sleep;
I cannot walk for utter weariness,
And I must rest a moment on this bank,
But let it not be long." As thus she spoke,
In half formed words, she sank on the smooth snow,
With closing lids. Her guide composed the robe
About her limbs, and said: "A pleasant spot
Is this to slumber in; on such a couch
Oft have I slept away the winter night,
And had the sweetest dreams." So Eva slept,
But slept in death; for when the power of frost

Locks up the motions of the living frame,
The victim passes to the realm of Death
Through the dim porch of Sleep. The little guide,
Watching beside her, saw the hues of life
Fade from the fair smooth brow and rounded cheek,
As fades the crimson from a morning cloud,
Till they were white as marble, and the breath
Had ceased to come and go, yet knew she not
At first that this was death. But when she marked
How deep the paleness was, how motionless
That once lithe form, a fear came over her.

She strove to wake the sleeper,
  plucked her robe,
And shouted in her ear, but all in
  vain;
The life had passed away from those
  young limbs.
Then the snow-maiden raised a wail-
  ing cry,
Such as the dweller in some lonely
  wild,
Sleepless through all the long Decem-
  ber night,
Hears when the mournful east begins
  to blow.
  But suddenly was heard the sound
    of steps,

Grating on the crisp snow; the cot-
  tagers
Were seeking Eva; from afar they
  saw
The twain, and hurried toward them.
  As they came
With gentle chidings ready on their
  lips,
And marked that deathlike sleep, and
  heard the tale
Of the snow-maiden, mortal anguish
  fell
Upon their hearts, and bitter words
  of grief
And blame were uttered: "Cruel,
  cruel one,

To tempt our daughter thus, and
  cruel we,
Who suffered her to wander forth
  alone
In this fierce cold!" They lifted the
  dear child,
And bore her home and chafed her
  tender limbs,
And strove, by all the simple arts
  they knew,
To make the chilled blood move, and
  win the breath
Back to her bosom; fruitlessly they
  strove;
The little maid was dead. In blank
  despair

They stood, and gazed at her who
  never more
Should look on them. "Why die we
  not with her?"
They said; "without her, life is
  bitterness."
  Now came the funeral-day; the
    simple folk
Of all that pastoral region gathered
  round
To share the sorrow of the cottagers.
They carved a way into the mound of
  snow
To the glen's side, and dug a little
  grave

In the smooth slope, and, following
the bier,
In long procession from the silent door,
Chanted a sad and solemn melody:

"Lay her away to rest within the
ground.
Yea, lay her down whose pure and
innocent life

Was spotless as these snows; for she
was reared
In love, and passed in love life's
pleasant spring,

And all that now our tenderest love
can do
Is to give burial to her lifeless
limbs."

They paused. A thousand slender
    voices round,
Like echoes softly flung from rock
    and hill,
Took up the strain, and all the
    hollow air
Seemed mourning for the dead; for,
    on that day,
The Little People of the Snow had
    come,
From mountain-peak, and cloud, and
    icy hall,
To Eva's burial. As the murmur died,
The funeral-train renewed the solemn
    chant:
    "Thou, Lord, hast taken her to be
    with Eve,
Whose gentle name was given her.
    Even so,
For so Thy wisdom saw that it was
    best
For her and us. We bring our bleed-
    ing hearts,
And ask the touch of healing from
    Thy hand,
As, with submissive tears, we render
    back
The lovely and beloved to Him who
    gave."
    They ceased. Again the plaintive
    murmur rose.
From shadowy skirts of low-hung
    cloud it came,
And wide white fields, and fir-trees
    capped with snow,
Shivering to the sad sounds. They
    sank away
To silence in the dim-seen distant
    woods.

The little grave was closed; the
    funeral-train
Departed; winter wore away; the
    Spring
Steeped, with her quickening rains,
    the violet-tufts,
By fond hands planted where the
    maiden slept.
But, after Eva's burial, never more
The Little People of the Snow were
    seen
By human eye, nor ever human
    ear
Heard from their lips articulate
    speech again;
For a decree went forth to cut them
    off,
Forever, from communion with man-
    kind.
The winter-clouds, along the moun-
    tain-side,
Rolled downward toward the vale,
    but no fair form
Leaned from their folds, and, in the
    icy glens,
And aged woods, under snow-loaded
    pines,
Where once they made their haunt,
    was emptiness.
    But ever, when the wintry days
    drew near,
Around that little grave, in the long
    night,
Frost-wreaths were laid and tufts of
    silvery rime
In shape like blades and blossoms of
    the field,
As one would scatter flowers upon a
    bier.

## ABRAHAM LINCOLN.

On, slow to smite and swift to spare,
  Gentle and merciful and just!
Who, in the fear of God, didst bear
  The sword of power, a nation's trust!

In sorrow by thy bier we stand,
  Amid the awe that hushes all,
And speak the anguish of a land
  That shook with horror at thy fall.

Thy task is done; the bond are free:
  We bear thee to an honored grave,
Whose proudest monument shall be
  The broken fetters of the slave.

Pure was thy life; its bloody close
  Hath placed thee with the sons of light,
Among the noble host of those
  Who perished in the cause of Right.

77

## A LEGEND OF ST. MARTIN.

Shrewd was the good St. Martin; he
 was famed
 For sly expedients and devices
  quaint;
And autumn's latest sunny days are
 named
 St. Martin's summer from the
  genial saint.
Large were his charities; one winter
 day
He saw a half-clad beggar in the way,
 And stopped and said: "Well met,
  my friend, well met;
That nose of thine, I see, is quite too
 blue."
With that his trenchant sword he
 drew—
 For he was in the service yet—
And cut his military cloak in two;
 And with a pleasant laugh
He bade the shivering rogue take
 half.

On one of the great roads of
 France
Two travellers were journeying on a
 day.
 The saint drew near, as if by
  chance,
And joined them, walking the same
 way.
A shabby pair in truth were they,
 For one was meanly covetous, and
  one
 An envious wretch—so doth the
  legend run.
Yet courteously they greeted him,
 and talked

Of current topics; for example,
 whether
There would be war, and what to-
 morrow's weather,
Cheating the weary furlongs as they
 walked.
 And when the eventide drew near
Thus spoke the saint: "We part to-
 night;
 I am St. Martin, and I give you
  here
The means to make your fortunes,
 used aright;
 Let one of you think what will
  please him best,
And freely ask what I will freely
 give.
And he who asks not shall from me
 receive
 Twice what the other gains by his
  request;
 And now I take my leave."
He spoke, and left the astonished
 men
Delighted with his words; but then
The question rose, which of that
 lucky pair
Should speak the wish and take the
 smaller share.
 Each begged the other not to heed
 The promptings of a selfish greed,
But frame at once, since he so well
 knew how,
The amplest, fullest wish that words
 allow.
 "Dear comrade, act a princely
  part;
 Lay every sordid thought aside;

Show thyself generous as thou
art;
Take counsel of thy own large
heart,
And nobly for our common good
provide."
But neither prayers nor flatteries
availed;
They passed from these to threats,
and threats too failed.
Thus went the pleadings on, until at
last
The covetous man, his very blood
on fire,
Flew at his fellow's throat and
clenched it fast,
And shrieked: "Die, then, or do
what I require;
Die, strangled like a dog." That
taunt awoke
A fierce anger in his envious
mate,

And merged the thirst of gain in
bitter hate;
And with a half-choked voice he
spoke,
Dissembling his malign intent,
"Take off thy hand and I con-
sent."
The grasp was loosened, and he
raised a shout,
"I wish that one of my own eyes
were out."
The wish was gratified as soon as
heard.
St. Martin punctually kept his word.
The envious man was one-eyed from
that day,
The other blind for his whole life
remained.
And this was all the good that
either gained
From the saint's offer in the public
way.

## THE WORDS OF THE KORAN.

EMIR HASSAN, of the prophet's race,
Asked with folded hands the Al-
mighty's grace.
Then within the banquet-hall he sat
At his meal upon the embroidered mat.

There a slave before him placed the
food,
Spilling from the charger, as he
stood,
Awkwardly, upon the Emir's breast,
Drops that foully stained the silken
vest.

To the floor, in great remorse and
dread,
Fell the slave, and thus beseeching
said:
"Master! they who hasten to re-
strain
Rising wrath, in Paradise shall
reign."

Gentle was the answer Hassan gave:
"I'm not angry." "Yet," pursued
the slave,
"Yet doth higher recompense be-
long
To the injured who forgives a
wrong."

"I forgive," said Hassan. "Yet we
read,"
Thus the prostrate slave went on to
plead,
"That a higher place in glory still
Waits the man who renders good for
ill."

"Slave, receive thy freedom, and be-
hold
In thy hands I lay a purse of gold;
Let me never fail to heed in aught
What the prophet of our God hath
taught."

81

6

## THE MYSTERY OF FLOWERS.

NOT idly do I stray
At prime, where far the mountain
ridges run,

And note, along my way,
Each flower that opens in the early
sun;

Or gather blossoms by the valley's
    spring,
When the sun sets and dancing in-
    sects sing.

Each has her moral rede,
Each of the gentle family of flowers;
    And I with patient heed,
Oft spell their lessons in my graver
    hours.
The faintest streak that on a petal lies,
May speak instruction to initiate eyes.

    Cummington, 1840.

And well do poets teach
Each blossom's charming mystery;
    declare,
    In clear melodious speech,
The silent admonitions pencilled
    there;
And from the Love of Beauty, aptly
    taught,
Lead to a higher good, the willing
    thought.

    Roslyn, 1875.

## THE CENTENNIAL HYMN.

THROUGH calm and storm the years
    have led
    Our nation on, from stage to
      stage—
A century's space—until we tread
    The threshold of another age.

We see where o'er our pathway
    swept
    A torrent-stream of blood and fire,
And thank the Guardian Power who
    kept
    Our sacred League of States entire.

Oh, chequered train of years, fare-
    well!
    With all thy strifes and hopes and
      fears!
Yet with us let thy memories dwell,
    To warn and teach the coming
      years.

And thou, the new-beginning age,
    Warned by the past, and not in
      vain,
Write on a fairer, whiter page,
    The record of thy happier reign.

## THE FLOOD OF YEARS.

A MIGHTY Hand, from an exhaustless
Urn,
Pours forth the never-ending Flood
of Years,
Among the nations. How the rush-
ing waves
Bear all before them! On their fore-
most edge,
And there alone, is Life. The Pres-
ent there
Tosses and foams, and fills the air
with roar
Of mingled noises. There are they
who toil,
And they who strive, and they who
feast, and they
Who hurry to and fro. The sturdy
swain—
Woodman and delver with the spade
—is there,
And busy artisan beside his bench,
And pallid student with his written
roll.
A moment on the mounting billow
seen,
The flood sweeps over them and they
are gone.
There groups of revellers whose
brows are twined
With roses, ride the topmost swell
awhile,
And as they raise their flowing cups
and touch
The clinking brim to brim, are
whirled beneath
The waves and disappear. I hear
the jar
Of beaten drums, and thunders that
break forth

From cannon, where the advancing
billow sends
Up to the sight long files of armèd
men,
That hurry to the charge through
flame and smoke.
The torrent bears them under,
whelmed and hid
Slayer and slain, in heaps of bloody
foam.
Down go the steed and rider, the
plumed chief
Sinks with his followers; the head
that wears
The imperial diadem goes down be-
side
The felon's with cropped ear and
branded cheek.
A funeral-train—the torrent sweeps
away
Bearers and bier and mourners. By
the bed
Of one who dies men gather sorrow-
ing,
And women weep aloud; the flood
rolls on;
The wail is stifled and the sobbing
group
Borne under. Hark to that shrill,
sudden shout,
The cry of an applauding multitude,
Swayed by some loud-voiced orator
who wields
The living mass as if he were its
soul!
The waters choke the shout and all is
still.
Lo! next a kneeling crowd, and one
who spreads

The hands in prayer—the engulfing wave o'ertakes
And swallows them and him. A sculptor wields
The chisel, and the stricken marble grows
To beauty; at his easel, eager-eyed,
A painter stands, and sunshine at his touch
Gathers upon his canvas, and life glows;
A poet, as he paces to and fro,
Murmurs his sounding lines. Awhile they ride
The advancing billow, till its tossing crest
Strikes them and flings them under, while their tasks
Are yet unfinished. See a mother smile
On her young babe that smiles to her again;
The torrent wrests it from her arms; she shrieks
And weeps, and midst her tears is carried down.
A beam like that of moonlight turns the spray
To glistening pearls; two lovers, hand in hand,
Rise on the billowy swell and fondly look
Into each other's eyes. The rushing flood
Flings them apart: the youth goes down; the maid
With hands outstretched in vain, and streaming eyes,
Waits for the next high wave to follow him.
An aged man succeeds; his bending form
Sinks slowly. Mingling with the sullen stream

Gleam the white locks, and then are seen no more.
Lo! wider grows the stream—a sea-like flood
Saps earth's walled cities; massive palaces
Crumble before it; fortresses and towers
Dissolve in the swift waters; populous realms
Swept by the torrent see their ancient tribes
Engulfed and lost; their very languages
Stifled, and never to be uttered more.
I pause and turn my eyes, and looking back
Where that tumultuous flood has been, I see
The silent ocean of the Past, a waste
Of waters weltering over graves, its shores
Strewn with the wreck of fleets where mast and hull
Drop away piecemeal; battlemented walls
Frown idly, green with moss, and temples stand
Unroofed, forsaken by the worshipper.
There lie memorial stones, whence time has gnawed
The graven legends, thrones of kings o'erturned,
The broken altars of forgotten gods,
Foundations of old cities and long streets
Where never fall of human foot is heard,
On all the desolate pavement. I behold
Dim glimmerings of lost jewels, far within

The sleeping waters, diamond, sardonyx,
Ruby and topaz, pearl and chrysolite,
Once glittering at the banquet on fair brows
That long ago were dust, and all around
Strewn on the surface of that silent sea
Are withering bridal wreaths, and glossy locks
Shorn from dear brows, by loving hands, and scrolls
O'er written, haply with fond words of love
And vows of friendship, and fair pages flung
Fresh from the printer's engine. There they lie
A moment, and then sink away from sight.
 I look, and the quick tears are in my eyes,
For I behold in every one of these
A blighted hope, a separate history
Of human sorrows, telling of dear ties
Suddenly broken, dreams of happiness
Dissolved in air, and happy days too brief
That sorrowfully ended, and I think
How painfully must the poor heart have beat
In bosoms without number, as the blow
Was struck that slew their hope and broke their peace.
 Sadly I turn and look before, where yet
The Flood must pass, and I behold a mist
Where swarm dissolving forms, the brood of Hope,
Divinely fair, that rest on banks of flowers,
Or wander among rainbows, fading soon
And reappearing, haply giving place
To forms of grisly aspect such as Fear
Shapes from the idle air — where serpents lift
The head to strike, and skeletons stretch forth
The bony arm in menace. Further on
A belt of darkness seems to bar the way
Long, low, and distant, where the Life to come
Touches the Life that is. The Flood of Years
Rolls toward it near and nearer. It must pass
That dismal barrier. What is there beyond?
Hear what the wise and good have said. Beyond
That belt of darkness, still the Years roll on
More gently, but with not less mighty sweep.
They gather up again and softly bear
All the sweet lives that late were overwhelmed
And lost to sight, all that in them was good,
Noble, and truly great, and worthy of love—
The lives of infants and ingenuous youths,
Sages and saintly women who have made
Their households happy; all are raised and borne
By that great current in its onward sweep,

Wandering and rippling with caress-
    ing waves
Around green islands with the breath
Of flowers that never wither. So
    they pass
Fr m stage to stage along the shining
    course
Of that bright river, broadening like
    a sea.
As its smooth eddies curl along their
    way
They bring old friends together;
    hands are clasped
In joy unspeakable; the mother's arms
Again are folded round the child she
    loved
And lost. Old sorrows are forgotten
    now,

Or but remembered to make sweet
    the hour
That overpays them; wounded hearts
    that bled
Or broke are healed forever. In the
    room
Of this grief-shadowed present, there
    shall be
A Present in whose reign no grief
    shall gnaw
The heart, and never shall a tender
    tie
Be broken; in whose reign the
    eternal Change
That waits on growth and action
    shall proceed
With everlasting Concord hand in
    hand.

## IN MEMORY OF JOHN LOTHROP MOTLEY.

SLEEP, Motley! with the great of ancient days,
   Who wrote for all the years that yet shall be;
Sleep with Herodotus, whose name and praise
   Have reached the isles of earth's remotest sea;
Sleep, while, defiant of the slow decays
   Of time, thy glorious writings speak for thee,
And in the answering heart of millions raise
   The generous zeal for Right and Liberty.
And should the day o'ertake us when, at last,
   The silence that, ere yet a human pen
Had traced the slenderest record of the past—
   Hushed the primeval languages of men—
Upon our English tongue its spell shall cast,
   Thy memory shall perish only then.

91

## THE TWENTY-SECOND OF FEBRUARY.

PALE is the February sky,
  And brief the mid-day's sunny
    hours;
The wind-swept forest seems to sigh
  For the sweet time of leaves and
    flowers.

Yet has no month a prouder day,
  Not even when the summer broods
O'er meadows in their fresh array,
  Or autumn tints the glowing
    woods.

For this chill season now again
  Brings, in its annual round, the
    morn
When, greatest of the sons of men,
  Our glorious Washington was born.

Lo, where, beneath an icy shield,
  Calmly the mighty Hudson flows!
By snow-clad fell and frozen field,
  Broadening, the lordly river goes.

The wildest storm that sweeps
    through space,
  And rends the oak with sudden
    force,
Can raise no ripple on his face,
  Or slacken his majestic course.

Thus, 'mid the wreck of thrones,
    shall live
  Unmarred, undimmed, our hero's
    fame,
And years succeeding years shall give
  Increase of honors to his name.

## FABLES.

### THE ELM AND THE VINE.

" UPHOLD my feeble branches
  By thy strong arms, I pray."
Thus to the Elm her neighbor
  The Vine was heard to say.
" Else, lying low and helpless,
  A wretched lot is mine,
Crawled o'er by every reptile,
  And browsed by hungry kine."
The Elm was moved to pity.
  Then spoke the generous tree:
" My hapless friend, come hither,
  And find support in me."
The kindly Elm, receiving
  The grateful Vine's embrace,
Became, with that adornment,
  The garden's pride and grace;
Became the chosen covert
  In which the wild-birds sing;
Became the love of shepherds,
  And glory of the spring.

Oh, beautiful example
  For youthful minds to heed!
The good we do to others
  Shall never miss its meed.
The love of those whose sorrows
  We lighten shall be ours;
And o'er the path we walk in
  That love shall scatter flowers.

### THE DONKEY AND THE MOCKING-BIRD.

A MOCK-BIRD in a village
  Had somehow gained the skill
To imitate the voices
  Of animals at will.

And, singing in his prison
  Once at the close of day,
He gave with great precision
  The donkey's heavy bray.

Well pleased, the mock-bird's mas-
    ter
  Sent to the neighbors round,
And bade them come together
  To hear that curious sound.

They came, and all were talking
  In praise of what they heard,
And one delighted lady
  Would fain have bought the
    bird.

A donkey listened sadly,
  And said : " Confess I must,
That these are stupid people,
  And terribly unjust.

" I'm bigger than the mock-bird,
  And better bray than he,
Yet not a soul has uttered
  A word in praise of me."

### THE CATERPILLAR AND THE BUTTERFLY.

#### (*Selected.*)

" GOOD-MORROW, friend." So spoke,
    upon a day,
  A caterpillar to a butterfly.
The winged creature looked another
    way,
  And made this proud reply:
" No friend of worms am I."

The insulted caterpillar heard,
And answered thus the taunting
    word;
  "And what wert thou, I pray,
Ere God bestowed on thee that brave
    array?
Why treat the caterpillar tribe with
    scorn?
  Art thou, then, nobly born?
What art thou, madam, at the best?
A caterpillar elegantly dressed."

### THE SPIDER'S WEB.

A DEXTROUS spider chose
The delicate blossom of a garden
    rose
Whereon to plant and bind
The net he framed to take the insect
    kind.
And when his task was done,
Proud of the cunning lines his art
    had spun,
He said: "I take my stand
Close by my work, and watch what I
    have planned.
And now, if Heaven should bless
My labors with but moderate success,
No fly shall pass this way,
Nor gnat, but they shall fall an easy
    prey."
He spoke, when from the sky
A strong wind swooped, and whirl-
    ing, hurried by,
And, far before the blast,
Rose, leaf, and web, and plans and
    hopes were cast.

### THE DIAL AND THE SUN.

A DIAL, looking from a stately
    tower,
  While from his cloudless path in
    heaven the Sun

Shone on its disk, as hour succeeded
    hour,
  Faithfully marked their flight till
    day was done.

Fair was that gilded disk, but when
    at last
  Night brought the shadowy hours
    'twixt eve and prime,
No longer that fair disk, for those
    who passed,
  Measured and marked the silent
    flight of time.

The human mind, on which no
    hallowed light
  Shines from the sphere beyond the
    starry train,
Is like the Dial's gilded disk at
    night,
  Whose cunning tracery exists in
    vain.

### THE EAGLE AND THE SERPENT.

A SERPENT watched an eagle gain,
  On soaring wings, a mountain
    height,
And envied him, and crawled with
    pain
  To where he saw the bird alight.
So fickle fortune oftentimes
  Befriends the cunning and the
    base,
And many a grovelling reptile climbs
  Up to the eagle's lofty place.

### THE WOODMAN AND SANDAL-TREE.

BESIDE a sandal-tree a woodman
    stood
  And swung the axe, and while
    its blows were laid

Upon the fragrant trunk, the generous wood
  With its own sweet perfumed the
  cruel blade.
Go, then, and do the like. A soul
endued
  With light from heaven, a nature
  pure and great,
Will place its highest bliss in doing
good,
  And good for evil give, and love
  for hate.

### THE HIDDEN RILL.

Across a pleasant field a rill unseen
  Glides from a fountain, nor does
  aught betray
Its presence, save a tint of lovelier
  green,

And flowers that scent the air
  along its way.
Thus silently should charity attend
  Those who in want's drear chambers pine and grieve;
No token should reveal the aid we
lend,
  Save the glad looks our welcome
  visits leave.

### THE COST OF A PLEASURE.

Upon the valley's lap
  The liberal morning throws
A thousand drops of dew
  To wake a single rose.

Thus often, in the course
  Of life's few fleeting years,
A single pleasure costs
  The soul a thousand tears.

96

CPSIA information can be obtained at www.ICGtesting.com
Printed in the USA
LVOW09s0227301113

363193LV00005B/231/P